The Trustworthy God

Pat Eastwell

authorHOUSE

AuthorHouse™ UK
1663 Liberty Drive
Bloomington, IN 47403 USA
www.authorhouse.co.uk
Phone: 0800.197.4150

© 2018 Pat Eastwell. All rights reserved.

No part of this book may be reproduced, stored in a retrieval system, or transmitted by any means without the written permission of the author.

Published by AuthorHouse 02/21/2018

ISBN: 978-1-5462-8402-4 (sc)
ISBN: 978-1-5462-8404-8 (e)

Library of Congress Control Number: 2018900874

Print information available on the last page.

Any people depicted in stock imagery provided by Thinkstock are models, and such images are being used for illustrative purposes only.
Certain stock imagery © Thinkstock.

This book is printed on acid-free paper.

Because of the dynamic nature of the Internet, any web addresses or links contained in this book may have changed since publication and may no longer be valid. The views expressed in this work are solely those of the author and do not necessarily reflect the views of the publisher, and the publisher hereby disclaims any responsibility for them.

Scripture quotations marked KJV are from the Holy Bible, King James Version (Authorized Version). First published in 1611. Quoted from the KJV Classic Reference Bible, Copyright © 1983 by The Zondervan Corporation.

Contents

Dedication ix
Acknowledgements xi
Foreword xiii

Chapter 1   Introduction 1
Chapter 2   My Own Conversion 4
Chapter 3   My Calling 9
Chapter 4   Miscellaneous Notes 11
Chapter 5   Protection 15
Chapter 6   Warfare Strategies 18
Chapter 7   Conversions 21
Chapter 8   Healing 25
Chapter 9   Financial Provision 29
Chapter 10 Failures 36
Chapter 11 Truth 40
Chapter 12 Opposition 45
Chapter 13 Angelic Help 50
Chapter 14 Witnessing 54
Chapter 15 Keeping Appointments 57
Chapter 16 Intercession 61
Chapter 17 "Selfisms" Notes 64
Chapter 18 Notes on Salvation 67

Chapter 19 Notes on Pride	72
Chapter 20 Notes on New Age Practices	76
Chapter 21 The Need for Ongoing Repentance	83
Chapter 22 Finale	84
Author Description	87

I will show forth all thy
marvellous works. (Psalm 9:1b)

Dedication

To all Christians who need encouragement to trust God more, and for them to have more revelation of His character, thereby strengthening their faith.

Acknowledgements

My thanks go to all who have given me encouragement in the past, even those who did so negatively, because, as a result, I prayed more and trusted Him more.

Thanks also go to all preachers who practised what they taught, setting an example to me.

Thanks also go to my publishers, who have guided me in the process of making this booklet available.

Last, but not least, my thanks to my faithful intercessor who wishes to remain anonymous.

All Bible quotations are from the King James Authorised Version.

Foreword

I offer this booklet for the Lord Jesus Christ to use as an encouragement for any Christian believer who may be feeling worn down by their life's circumstances. In our Father God's mercy, I pray they find their focus renewed on Him.

Unbelievers may also seek within this booklet to better enable them in their decision about choosing Jesus as their own Saviour and Lord.

Most chapters are examples of following the Holy Spirit's promptings. Other chapters are notes offered on topics which some church attendees may not previously have examined, supported by scriptural remedies. All chapters have a short prayer to end.

And any glory goes to the Lord Jesus Christ. Amen

1
Introduction

I had attended a women's conference on emotional wholeness, at which there were two workshops. The conference was based on Psalm 37:3–4: "Trust in the Lord, and do good; so shalt thou dwell in the land, and verily then thou shalt be fed. Delight thyself also in the Lord; and he shall give thee the desires of thine heart."

Both workshops took place at the same time—one on "Trust" and the other on "Doing Good". In my room during the break beforehand, I prayed for guidance as to which one to attend. I felt the Holy Spirit say, "Read Psalm 16," which I did. The first verse of that psalm said, "Preserve me, O God: for in thee do I put my trust." As the Holy Spirit seemed to indicate that I was already trusting Him, I decided to go to the workshop on "Doing Good". It turned out that my expectation was a bit askew; I thought maybe opportunities for doing good would be outlined. No, the workshop was for delegates to share how the Lord Jesus Christ had challenged individuals to step out in faith and do ... whatever.

I scanned my memory in order to share something, but by the time I had chosen something, time had run out. I had misplaced expectations for opportunities for service being aired because six years previously I had moved to the area and was now attending my fifth church! Church hopping, as it has been called, is not part of my belief system (with hindsight after you have read this booklet it will hopefully become clearer why the powers that be in those five churches were not comfortable with me). Yet I took comfort from my daily readings which seemed to focus on the Lord hedging me in for His purposes. If He was happy with my interceding and praying, I could hardly complain. Yielding to His purposes, I assumed, was His agenda for me at that time, and He would open a door for service in His time.

So back to the conference: the penultimate session on the Sunday morning, ended with the phrase "being made emotionally whole, so that …"(the "so that" would be individual for each person). "Lord," I said, "the 'so that' is missing for me." I went for prayer, asking for agreement that the Lord would soon show me what the "so that" would be for me.

Back home the next morning as I reflected on this conference workshop and my difficulty in choosing a memory, I prayed, "Father, I am sorry I did not contribute. There were so many memories I could have shared, I did not know where to start."

I felt the Holy Spirit say, "Categorize them," which I did.

"See what I mean, Lord; there is enough here to fill … (and as I completed the sentence, the Holy Spirit joined me) … "a book." These categories form the different chapter headings, and each ends with a prayer. So dip into various chapters for encouragement on its topic, or take in the whole booklet for a boost to appreciating the character of our Christian God. For those who may be doubtful about the Christian faith, may this booklet encourage them to go on to accept the Lord Jesus Christ as their own Saviour.

Prayer

Lord, for those who read the ensuing, I pray their faith in Your trustworthiness of God will increase, and may more hope arise to see You work in their own lives. Amen.

2

My Own Conversion

I was born with no natural advantages: breech birth (for which I took personal responsibility, until I renounced that viewpoint); on a social housing estate; of a dysfunctional family line; during post-war rationing, a period of poverty; evacuated with my mother at six weeks of age to Scotland (I found out in my adulthood that our landlady was a spiritualist!); and of probable Jewish extraction (but this only came to light years later and was not known to my immediate forebears).

When I was about five years of age, my parents attended a Kingdom Hall for a time; but that did not last long. I must have committed some minor misdemeanour, because one of the ladies said to me, "Mr. Russell would not like that."

I asked, "Who is Mr. Russell?"

"Oh, he is dead now."

I retorted, "He will be unaware of it then." Was this the start of my antithesis to peer pressure?

Attendance there came to an abrupt end when my younger brother and I were enrolled for an outing on our own with the other children. On the day of departure my mother was told that my brother was too young to go. My mother reacted with "I'm not wasting all my money, so you are still going." I sat on the bus sobbing. A married couple took me under their wing for the day, but this mix-up was the catalyst for my parents to leave.

All this spiritual legacy could have alienated me from Father God, but He had other ideas. At my first Christmas at school, aged nearly six, we sang some carols. The second verse of 'Away in a Manger' impacted me, making me tearful; the line which requested we be fit to live with God in heaven was the trigger for my upset. Many years later, I shared a teenage photo of myself and some family members with a friend. "You look really serious," she said. To which I replied, "Life was serious."

Do not assume that I had qualities which moved God to favour me. It has all been His doing, by His grace. Deuteronomy 9:5 reads, "Not for thy righteousness, or for the uprightness of thine heart, dost thou [Israel] go to possess the land but ... that he [God]may perform the word which the Lord sware unto thy fathers, Abraham, Isaac, and Jacob."

However, my mother was quietly becoming worried about me by my early teens. I had withdrawn into studying so I could later escape the lifestyle of the estate where we lived. She suggested I go to a girls' club at a church hall near us, thinking I needed friends. It turned out that this club was a branch of the Christian group called the Girl Covenanters.

A few weeks after joining, we all went to the annual conference in the Albert Hall, London (there were six of us and two helpers). We were on the top balcony, which gave us a good view over everything. As I looked at the vast choir and the packed auditorium, I thought to myself, *These Christians can't all be mad.* God had started to plough up the hard ground, in preparation for my eventual salvation.

A month or two later, an invitation was given by the group leaders to attend an evangelist's meeting: I alone of the six said I would go, just to have an evening away from home. A leader and I went together.

The evangelist (whose name I had never heard of) was in full Royal Air Force uniform. He described his difficulties in meeting the criteria to get admitted to the RAF, even though his own father had been in the RAF before him. First, the evangelist had to have two attempts at the entrance exam. Then he failed the medical exam, being too overweight. He next started to slim and was reweighed, but failed again. Then he started exercising to aid the dieting and was reweighed, but failed again. Then he added hot bathing to his regime in the hope of sweating off more weight, still dieting and exercising as well. This time he had a borderline result, and one of the recruiters said to the other, "You know So-and-so, who is in the RAF—he is overweight. I think we should let this one in."

All of this evangelist's efforts went to prove, he said, that by our own means we do not get into heaven: not by parental faith, inheritance, or hard work. He ended his talk with "So if you feel you do not fit in and are unloved, consider Jesus." I made a will choice, rather than an emotional one, and followed in saying the sinner's prayer, repenting of my sins in general. Later, Father God led me to be more specific over some sins. On exiting the meeting, I asked myself, *What have I done? I have given control* of my life to Jesus. Well, I have done it, and that is that. There is no going back now.

On the bus journey home, I was asked whether I had decided for Jesus yet. I said, "Yes, at the Albert Hall," (the reason being I wanted to inform my parents first).

When I entered our house, my mother asked, "Did you have a good time?"

"Yes, I have become a Christian." (I was the first one to do so in our family. In case you are wondering, years later my parents came to the Lord at different times.)

Years later, someone from the pulpit asked the question, "Who prayed you into the kingdom?" When I asked Father God, He showed me a memory of my mother's ex-boss (whose employment she had left to have me). This ex-boss was an orthodox Jew. I believe Father God was telling me that this ex-boss had prayed the Aaronic blessing over me. I guess he and his wife had spiritual discussions with my mother, to which I was not privy.

Then one day, he was gone—a fatal stroke. I felt abandoned. This had been a childless couple, and my brother and I had had a special place in their hearts. My mother continued to keep in touch with the widowed wife, until the day years later, a nursing home wrote and said she had passed away.

That is my conversion: the fruit being that I immediately stopped swearing.

Prayer

Father God, I pray for those readers who may still be searching for the truth, yet do not equate that truth with the Lord Jesus Christ. Please, Father God, enlighten their understanding by removing any veil darkening their spiritual perceptions so that they will have the knowledge of the spiritual inheritance You have promised to those who believe in You. Amen

"That the God of our Lord Jesus Christ, the Father of glory, may give unto you the spirit of wisdom and revelation in the knowledge of Him: the eyes of your understanding being enlightened; that ye may know what is the hope of his calling, and what the riches of the glory of his inheritance in the saints; and what is the exceeding greatness of his power to us-ward who believe, according to the working of his mighty power …."(Ephesians 1:17–19)

3
My Calling

"For the gifts and calling of God are without repentance." (Romans 11:29)

1 Having just started a new job, for the first six Mondays I had to attend an occupational therapy college for awareness training. Whilst driving the forty-five-minute journey to the college, I was reviewing the sermon preached the previous day. The pastor had preached on the ministry gifts from 1 Corinthians 12. I wonder what mine is, I mused.

The Holy Spirit answered, "You are part of My 'mopping up brigade'. Make yourself available to Me, and I will bring people across your path." (I did not see the words 'mopping-up brigade' in actual print until years later; those in this brigade are Christians whom God calls to the deliverance ministry.)

2 At the same church, at the cell group I attended, the leader said that he had not had time to prepare, so we would wait on the Lord for a word or picture, something symbolic of what the Lord wanted to give us, indicative of our calling. Father God showed me that I was in a standing position, holding to my chest a mirror with the reflective side away from myself. The ornate frame made of gold. It stretched from the bridge of my feet (not the floor) to my shoulders, yet there was no weight to it for my arms to bear. The leader asked if I knew what it meant. I replied, "Something to do with praying for people."

The reply followed: "Yes, and in addition there is a call to holy living. When people get near you, they will see if they fall short of holiness themselves. You may find 'friends' will melt into the background because of it though." My understanding of the Christian lifestyle was that we were all called to live holy lives, so this was no bigger challenge for me than what we all had. Of course, if I was called to the deliverance ministry, then this would depend on the level of holiness I was living in.

Yet as the years have rolled by, 'friends' have slipped away one by one. I have had to release them to the Lord.

Prayer

Father God, I pray for those who are awaiting their own calling from You for an opportunity to serve in Your church: strengthen their patience, and give them Your discernment for when the door of opportunity opens. Grant them a good support network. Amen.

4
Miscellaneous Notes

I give some personal thoughts on ideas I have come across in my fifty-nine years as a Christian and ministering to the body of Christ for some seven years.

1 "I am the good shepherd, and know my sheep, and am known of mine." (John 10:14)

The Lord Jesus Christ said the above: He guards us, feeds us, shelters us, and rescues us. Isaiah 49:16 says, "Behold, I have graven thee upon the palms of my hands …." Notice the singular pronoun 'thee'—yet another indication of the need to have a personal relationship with the Lord Jesus Christ. He cannot forget us; there is a constant reminder on the palms of His hands, through the nail piercing of the cross. This verse should not be used to justify tattooing as I once heard—that reason would clash with Deuteronomy 14:1 (not to cut the body) and Leviticus 19:28 (not to print marks on the body).

His palms bear the crucifixion nail marks as memory joggers (John 20:27). When we believe in the efficacy of His crucifixion and accept Him as our own Saviour and Lord, then we are accepted in the Beloved (Ephesians 1:6). He also knows who are His (Nahum 1:7; 2 Timothy 2:19). The only things He wants to forget are the sins we repent of: "As far as the east is from the west, so far has He removed our transgressions from us"(Psalm 103:12KJV). And we can never reach the horizon when travelling around the earth! "Jesus Christ [is] the same yesterday, and today, and forever"(Hebrews 13:8), and our task is "not laying again the foundation of repentance from dead works, and of faith toward God" (Hebrews 6:1).

Prayer

Father God, please encourage all of us to get the foundation of our Christian faith correct. If any were converted in a hurry via emotionalism or under pressure from any other human being and did not make their own choice under the influence of Your Holy Spirit (John 16:8–11), please bring clarity if need be, and fulfil what might be missing. Amen.

2 The Bible version I use is the King James Authorized Version. According to Deuteronomy 17:18–20, when the king makes his own copy of the Lord's word and consults it regularly, then that king will be working from the same "hymn sheet" as the priests. It is also easier to see from this version who it refers to with either *you* (plural) or *thee/thou* (singular). Ecclesiastes 8:4 says, "Where the word of a king is, there is power: and who may say unto him, What doest thou?" The King James Authorized Version, therefore, carries the power of King James.

And for the reader to check, how does John 11 v 27 read in the version you use? The King James Authorised Version reads: "She saith unto him, Yea, Lord: I believe that thou art the Christ, the Son of God, which should come into the world."

Prayer

Father God, I pray for those who want to read the King James Authorised version, but who may feel they would struggle with the language. Some translators of twentieth-century versions are reported to have attended séances. If such is the case, help us to repent if using a twentieth-century version, as there could be spiritual interference affecting the choice of version. Amen.

[For more on this subject, see *New Age Bible Versions* by G.A.Riplinger via www.avpublications.com or 1-800-435-4535.]

3 Some thoughts on the length of years we could expect to live: their Lord reduced Israel's life length because of their sin, down to seventy years (Numbers 14:30; Psalm 90:10). Saying things like "we have to expect a bit of illness as we get older" or "living on borrowed time" after reaching seventy years of age could become self-fulfilling prophecies. Do we really want to align ourselves with sinful Israel in their desert wanderings?

Psalm 92:14 says, "They shall still bring forth fruit in old age …." (Postscript—I wrote this booklet in my fifty-ninth year of Christianity.)

Prayer

Father God, scripture says we need to look for Your return (Hebrews 9:28). Please help us: "So teach us to number our days, that we may apply our hearts unto wisdom" (Psalm 90:12), so that we may finish the course You set for each of us. Amen.

4 Do you have a favourite ministry or person which has spoken to you, giving you prophetic direction to your life? According to Exodus 18:23, God should still have the last word, and we need to have any prophecy confirmed by Him: as was indicated by Moses' father-in-law in his reply to Moses' being overworked by the people; in effect, Moses was told to also check with God.

Prayer

Father God, if I have come under the influence of any prophetic word which I have straight away acted upon, and not waited for confirmation from You, I repent, and I ask You to undo any negative repercussions which followed. Amen.

5
Protection

Second Chronicles 16:9 says, "The eyes of the Lord run to and fro throughout the whole earth, to show himself strong in the behalf of them whose heart is perfect toward him"(*perfect* could also mean "loyal" or "at peace with").

1 We were due to go on holiday to the UK south coast, the route having been chosen the previous night. During my quiet time on the day of the departure, the Holy Spirit told me we were not to go via the already-chosen route. "Oh help, I am going with a non-believer who will be driving. Please confirm, Lord, what You have just told me."

"Read Matthew 2:13." Joseph was told to escape out of Israel. I also prayed that if there were to be a road accident on the first-chosen route, that there would be no loss of life. I explained to the driver, as mildly as I could, that we would need to go via another route. Needless to say, every red light or delay we encountered was met with his negative comment.

We took our designated seats for the evening meal. The couple who were seated next to us complained that their journey had taken longer than planned, due to a road accident (they had travelled on our first-chosen route). I asked if there had been any fatalities and was told no.

2 Someone I trusted received an invitation to another family's retirement meal. I was invited too (there would be six of us in total). However, the Holy Spirit said I was not to eat there. My reply was along the lines of "That would start World War III, so You will just have to protect me, because I need to respect these people." (I supposed the problem would be a possible case of food poisoning.) I prayed in tongues mentally all the way through the meal. To me the whole atmosphere seemed false and coercive. (I need to be sketchy over details as some attendees are still alive at the time of writing this booklet.)

On my return home, I repented of my disobedience in eating there and asked the Lord what it was all about. His reply indicated that I had been in great physical danger. In the Lord's mercy the only effect I had had was a thirst and sweating; nor did my muscle tone or mental functioning deteriorate. Praise His name.

Later, when I was living in a refuge place, my then pastor had gone to South Africa for a conference and had been billeted in a dormitory with a Christian South African detective. My pastor shared my story and my symptoms with this detective, who went back to his office and returned with a magazine article on different drugs. There my symptoms were confirmed.

3 On a holiday in Jersey, a crossing was booked from that island to Guernsey via the hydrofoil. On the day of departure there was a brisk storm, yet the authorities deemed the hydrofoil could cope, even though the ordinary ferry was cancelled. Out on open water, the hydrofoil was lifted up and down. In fact, as I looked out the window, sometimes the waves were so high that they obscured the sky. I reasoned that if Paul could cope, the Lord would help me as well. I practised the trick of pushing alternatively with my feet to mimic my body walking and prayed in tongues. Even some crew were travel sick.

On our arrival, those who had been travel sick were advised to go to a certain pharmacy on the waterfront, as they had a medication to settle upset stomachs. Some passengers flew back to Jersey! When asked why I had not been sick, I just smiled.

Prayer

Father God, I pray in Jesus' name that Your church will see in these dark days, that we do not battle with people (even though they may be enemy agents) but ultimately against the devil and his troop of fallen angels. Convince us afresh, Lord, that through the cross, the Lord Jesus Christ has won the final victory. Amen.

6
Warfare Strategies

Sadly, I have discerned wolves in sheep's clothing (Acts 20:29) within some church organizations, which proved correct by their fruit (Matthew 7:20. Opposition can come from within, as Jesus faced in Luke 4:34, or from without.

During my Christian lifetime, a strategy has been developed through which we can counter the enemy. I share this with the readers now:

1. We need to repent, if prompted by the Holy Spirit, which will restore our favourable standing with God (Acts 3:19).
2. We also need to forgive any human enemy and bless them (Matthew 5:44, where our Lord tells us to love and bless those who deliberately malign us).
3. Only then can we ask God to block any misuse of our own identifying information or even DNA (photos, car number plates, even stray hairs), which may give unclean spirits an "address" to target (Matthew 12:44, where our Lord indicates that the unclean spirit returns from where it had been evicted).

4. We need to keep our own home clean, so that the Holy Spirit does not depart (Romans 8: 11 where we are told that Holy Spirit dwells in us).
5. We could, if prompted by the Holy Spirit, anoint the boundary of our property as a rededication, again so the Holy Spirit does not depart (2 Chronicles 15:18 – where Asa renewed the altar).
6. We should vet who enters our homes and, after they depart, evict any unclean spirit that they may have brought with them (some people will not be aware they have any). This is not a judgement on them; rather, it is good "spiritual housekeeping" (1 John 1:5).
7. Honour God by tithing, making Him Lord in the financial arena. Not to tithe is to rob God (Malachi 3:8).
8. Check that spiritual armour has not been weakened (Ephesians6:10–18), and do any necessary repairs.
9. Eliminate doubting (1 Timothy 2:8).
10. Break any curses being sent, and evict the unclean spirits accompanying these curses (to ensure the curse "works"; Jeremiah 30:17). This is similar to issuing a higher decree than the enemy has issued; see Esther 8:8.
11. Do not fear - we have been given authority (Luke 9:1).
12. Attend a fellowship of like-minded Christians, to be built up and encouraged (Ephesians 4:12).
13. Praying in tongues (1 Corinthians 14:4) will keep enemies confused (1 Corinthians 2:11).

14. If prompted, fast, but not on the day of any expected attack. Fasting as a general part of our defences will deal with the unexpected (Ezra 8:23).
15. There is no armour for our backs; we are meant to be moving forward. Instead, when attacked there, the joy of the Lord will be a covering (strength) (Nehemiah 8:10).
16. When queuing, do not let confidential information pass into the air waves for enemies to use against us (Proverbs 29:11).
17. After all the above, give a shout of victory like Joshua, so as to glorify our Lord and Saviour.
18. Receiving gifts from people whose true motives we don't know could pave the way for other influences to enter our lives.

7

Conversions

1 I was leading a Sunday school group, and a visiting 12 year old lad was attending for one week, whose parents were on holiday and in the main congregation. Leading the group through the planned notes, the visiting lad questioned "I get this stuff about Jesus being on trial instead of us, but I don't understand the trinity". I answered "it's like we say that the Smith family live at a certain house address: so the God family live at a house called 'Trinity'. Keep it simple I thought. He understood and chose to become a Christian. He informed me later that his dad was a lawyer.

2 My pastor at the time years ago, was on a mission trip away, and I offered to go with his wife to visit his mother in the nursing home, which I had done before so I was not a total stranger to the mother. The night previous to the visit I dreamed of the impending visit, and the Lord said that I'd forgotten my training. (Just to explain, although the mother could talk well, her thought processes were becoming impaired and what the Lord was implying was that I had not drawn on my awareness training for dementia.) I shared the dream with the Pastor's wife.

When we arrived, there were no staff in the small day room. I pulled up a dining chair to be in front of the mother in order to keep her attention from wandering. I started by saying, "It is time to prepare to meet your Maker." (She was of an age when this would have been a common phrase.)I followed with "Repeat after me then … I am sorry –"

But at this point she interrupted me with "I am sorry for all the trouble I have caused you. Amen." I looked at the pastor's wife, who nodded. She thought this was sufficient.

Another resident who had been listening said, "I have always wanted to meet him," so a double harvest came in that day.

Three weeks later, the mother had a stroke and was confined to bed, almost incoherent.

3 My own widowed father came to live with us, after he had been told he had terminal cancer of the oesophagus (but see also the next chapter, on healing). He was not a believer, and the Lord told me to "snatch him from the fire" (Jude 23). The difficulty was that Father was also in the early stages of dementia, yet he was willing to come to church with me, since he enjoyed car journeys. I used to pray for a window of opportunity to witness to him, because he would fall asleep during church services.

One Sunday, the pastor said he had been led to preach on hell. Father stayed awake all through this sermon. On the way home, I asked him where he thought he would go. He answered, "I suppose I'll find out when I get there". *Some teaching that had gone awry*, I thought, so I said to him, "Dad that is not how it works. We all have to choose before we die, so I do not know where that idea came from." We came to a lay-by, and I pulled in and parked the car. "What are you going to choose?" He chose to go to heaven, and I led him to the Lord.

When we returned home, I asked the Lord for a sign of the reality of my father's conversion, as I did not want us to be tricked by dementia. When *Songs of Praise* came on the television that evening, whilst seemingly dozing and without opening his eyes, he sang the entire first verse of a well-known hymn. The next evening, he would not even smile at a joke putting down women that someone wanted to share with him.

4 One more example: I gave my testimony to a group of non-Christian ladies, who were on holiday funded by a Christian charity. At the end a lady approached me. She had been brought up with her mother and grandmother, both practising psychics. They may also have taken her to their local "services". She asked, "Can your Jesus silence the voices in my head? There is so much 'traffic' I can hardly think straight. And people tell me they feel uncomfortable with me because I put a damper on things."

I replied, "Jesus can if you believe in Him."

"Well, I liked your testimony and how Jesus protected you, so I will give Jesus a try." I led her to the Lord. Her Christian leader and I ministered to her and told the unclean psychic spirits to leave. At the end she sat quietly with her eyes shut for so long that we gently asked if she was OK. "I am enjoying the silence; all the 'traffic' has gone." Jesus said, "Peace I leave with you, my peace I give unto you: not as the world giveth, give I unto you" (John 14:27).

There have been other conversions, but these four depict one of the youngest and one of the oldest, and also one where spiritual opposition needed to be cut through. First Peter 3:15 admonishes us to "be ready always to give an answer to every man that asketh you a reason of the hope that is in you with meekness and fear."

Prayer

Father God, help us to love the lost, to recognize the genuine searcher after Your truth, and to be ready to follow the Holy Spirit when appointments for salvation arise. Amen.

8
Healing

"Is it not [the fast that I have chosen] to deal thy bread to the hungry, and that thou bring the poor that are cast out to thy house? when thou seest the naked, that thou cover him; and that thou hide not thyself from thine own flesh? Then shall thy light break forth as the morning, and thine health shall spring forth speedily ...." (Isaiah 58:7–8)

After a doctor's check for my father, due to his losing weight and his memory deteriorating, we went together to the hospital for further tests. The result was that there was cancer of the oesophagus, and I had been allowed to watch with him, with my own eyes, the video of their camera searching for the prognosis. The treatment prescribed was that a "stent" tube would be inserted within his own oesophagus to prevent it being closed by the cancer growth, thus starving him. I pleaded with the Lord, "He cannot die yet; he is not a believer."

After the operation to insert the tube, he was discharged to my care to build up his strength prior to returning to his own home. A church couple we knew invited us for a snack meal the next weekend at midday. "We are having soup, which will be fine for your dad." However, sandwiches came with the soup, and Dad, not remembering that we had been warned that bread could clog the tube, took a sandwich. Mentally, I prayed, "Lord I cannot tell him in front of these people that he cannot have that sandwich—he will feel criticized."

The Lord answered, "Shut up and have faith."

That got my attention. But the couple were sending me a questioning look, so I said, "Maybe the Lord is healing him." They raised their eyebrows, yet the sandwich was eaten.

Later that evening, back home, I reasoned that if the Lord had healed him, then I did not have to "drown" his cooked dinner with gravy. Another family member asked me the reason for the revised meal presentation. "He will be fine," I replied. And he was.

Some months later, my father developed a catarrhal cough, so yet another x-ray was taken. This time I was not allowed to see the result: a report would be sent to our medical practitioner, my father having opted to stay with us permanently. I went on my own to the doctor, and he said, "I am going to read the letter I have received, and see what you make of it: 'There is no abnormality in the chest cavity except for a stent tube'" (i.e. no cancer). Praise the Lord!

"Don't worry about it," I replied; "the prayer team have been on the case."

"Well, something has obviously happened. Now about this cough, I suggest …."

Thus, Father God gave my earthly father another six months to live, during which time at age eighty-three he came to know the Lord as his own personal Saviour.

2 We had been to Corfu half-board at a hotel the year before, and we were going back self-catering. The reason for the self-catering decision was that I had had multiple food allergies for ten years and could better monitor my food intake. My doctor did prescribe antihistamine to ward off some of the milder reactions, but this medication dulled my thinking and could not ease the worst symptoms.

The week before this return holiday I had attended a church teaching on the Holy Spirit, which was something we had not much of via normal church sermons. I bought the outside speaker's book on the subject for reading in the event of any airport delays. In the aeroplane halfway across Europe, one page cited Mark 16:17–18; and the page following cited the same verses. I shut my eyes "Lord, I am a believer so why is it that cows' milk is a poison to me?"

"You do not have to have it."

"What do I do with it then?"

"Put it at the foot of the cross." Mentally I did just that. At that point, still with my eyes shut, I had a vision of a golden shaft of light coming towards me from a great distance away, and it went right through me. There was no physical reaction to this, except that my eyes watered.

We arrived at the lodgings at 1.00 in the morning. I asked the Lord to prevent the other person from asking me how I was for three days, by which time I would have passed the gluten reaction time. In the meantime, I would take no antihistamine. The Lord arranged those three waiting days.

When I was asked how I was faring with the antihistamine, I replied, "I am not taking it; I was healed on the aeroplane."

"You cannot have been healed on the aeroplane; I was with you."

"Well, I was." As of the writing of this booklet, all this took place twenty-six years ago.

3 I was in Thailand as part of a mission team trip. At the end of some teaching by others, attendees were offered prayer. One lady (with her husband) came to me and said she could not read the Bible. "Is your eyesight poor, or is it something else?" I queried.

"No, I can read other books, but with the Bible the letters keep moving," she answered. She confirmed she was a Christian. I anointed her with oil and told anything unclean to leave in Jesus' name. I then gave her my Bible and said, "Read." She did with a big smile. We praised and thanked the Lord.

Prayer

Father God, Your timing can seem so strange to us, yet You have a right time for Your dealings with us. Help us to trust You more and more, to pursue the right way to live before You, and to persist in prayer. Amen

9

Financial Provision

A To Others

"As we have therefore opportunity, let us do good unto all men, especially unto them who are of the household of faith." (Galatians 6:10)

1 I was travelling westwards in the UK one summer, a trip I had travelled before, so I knew where to break the journey and get more petrol. I also took a packed lunch and a Christian book for the break in the journey. The book was on the subject of being obedient to the Holy Spirit's promptings.

Having filled the car with petrol, I settled down in my car to my lunch and my reading. I reached a challenging point in the narrative, where the author related something the Holy Spirit had told him to do. I looked up out of the car front window, saying to Him "I do not think I could do that."

At that point, I noticed a family about thirty metres away, picnicking. The father had obviously eaten and was dozing, whilst the mother was giving a jar of food to a very young child in a baby seat, at the same time keeping an eye on a little girl. The Holy Spirit said, "That is a Christian family, and I want you to give them £X."

"Lord, I do not know if I have £X left after paying cash for the petrol." I checked my purse, and I had the amount specified. So now the question of my obedience arose. One cannot read a book on obedience to the *rhema* word of God and then plead lack of courage. I went over to the other. "I am sorry to disturb you, but can I ask if you are Christians?" (If not, then no cash gift, I deduced.)

"Yes, we are."

"In that case, I need to give you this."

The father then sat up, having heard adult voices nearby. "Hello," he said to me.

I explained, "I was just telling your wife –"

What was his reaction? "You read about this in books, but never expect it to happen to oneself. Cannot wait to tell my dad, he is always pooh-poohing our faith. I was also wondering how we were going to manage financially through to the end of the month."

I wished them a safe journey to their holiday, and went back to my car. "That was stretching, Lord," I commented.

I settled back to read again. Then the mother knocked on my car window, whilst passing back to their car, and said, "I think you are very brave."

"I don't know about that, but look at the title of the book I have been reading. I could not wriggle out of it."

2 At a church I attended decades ago, a member's car failed to pass its motor worthiness check and had to be scrapped. The Lord told me to give £X. "That would not be enough for them to buy another car, Lord," I argued.

"Still give." I arranged for the money to go via the elders to preserve confidentiality. I heard later that when the recipients had told their unbelieving parents, the parental reaction was that they could do better than Christians and added to the sum double the amount I had been told to give. This new total bought a replacement car.

3 When the Iron Curtain stood in Eastern Europe, a church member was part of a mission group smuggling support for Christians into that area. On one occasion, Holy Spirit told me to give £X to this contact for a "forgotten church". Departure for the trip would be on a Tuesday, so at the Sunday morning service before, the trip agenda was given out. *Well, none of those could be termed "forgotten" and hardly a gap to fit anything unexpected in,* I commented to myself.

At the evening service, the announcement was made that at the Lord's insistence, the agenda had been abandoned! Having flexible working hours, I extended my lunch break on the Monday, visited a bank, and then called on the pastor. I gave him cash to pass on with a covering typed note (unsigned for confidentiality) to give to the "forgotten church".

Post the mission trip, feedback as given: one of the known Eastern European pastors had made an impromptu visit, requesting prayer for a situation he was in. As well as his own church, he was visiting a village (which had no church presence) and had purchased a piece of land to build one. This village was two hours' drive away by car from his own home. The missionaries identified this as the "forgotten church". In the Christian pastor's eyes that may have been the case, but not in Father God's eyes. On receiving the financial gift, he wept with gratitude to God and revealed that he had been fasting for a breakthrough.

Luke 14:29–30 says, "Lest haply, after he hath laid the foundation, and is not able to finish it, all that behold it begin to mock him, saying, This man began to build and was not able to finish …."

Previous to this, my own mother had died, and trips with my widowed father had taken place to all the various offices and banks needed under these circumstances. When her estate had been settled, my father gave me a cash gift in thanks for my support—the exact amount I had given away!

B To Myself

"Bring ye all the tithes into the storehouse, that there may be meat in mine house, and prove me now herewith, saith the Lord of Hosts, if I will not open you the windows of heaven, and pour you out a blessing, that there shall not be room enough to receive it." (Malachi 3:10–11)

1 "Change your car," instructed the Holy Spirit.

"But I am giving up working in order to care for my father.

I cannot borrow to buy another car, because I will not be able to fund any repayments." His instruction was repeated.

I recruited a (non-Christian) family member who was knowledgeable about second-hand cars. One car was seen in the local Saturday weekly newspaper, and we arranged to go and inspect the car. It was suggested we go on Sunday morning. "No, I will be at church then."

"It will be gone by the afternoon."

"I am still going to church."

The identified car was still unsold when we arrived, and we took the car for a test drive. As the preliminary discussion about my existing car's value had left a shortfall, I was still telling Father God that I could not borrow any money to fund the purchase. As we parked the potential replacement car, I saw a man looking around my car which I hoped to trade in. To the salesman I said, "I could sell to him privately and get more from a member of the public; that would cover the funding difference."

"You cannot do that, he is a dealer." These two went into a business discussion, while we had a coffee.

Praise the Lord — our salesman arranged to sell my existing car straight through the dealership books, doing no extra work on it, then on out again to this dealer. By discounting the dealership in-house work, my existing car went up in value, and I bought outright the replacement car we had just test-driven. The family member who had come with me could only keep repeating, "You are a jammy devil" in the world's vernacular.

2 After being put through a divorce, I was led by the Holy

Spirit and confirmed by my pastor at the time to go to a Christian training centre in Southern England. In the course of time, I was invited to join the team. I also had the impression from the Holy Spirit that He wanted me to buy a house in the area for the other students to rent, thus investing the divorce settlement. "Father, that would mean at the end of the mortgage term, I would need to find a lump sum to repay the capital," thus stating the obvious.

"Still buy" was His reply, and I obeyed.

In due course, and within the life of the mortgage, the Holy Spirit told me to return to the Eastern part of England, from where I had moved, which was also confirmed by two different Christians who shared pictures with me, and only I knew the meaning of them. During the few years I had owned the terraced house, prices had gone up in that area, and Eastern England was a slightly cheaper region.

I reckoned that now I was retiring, sense dictated to buy outright and not have a mortgage at all. The only house I could afford had just been reduced—but would still stretch my financial situation. I asked Father God for a sign. "I only want to buy a property that is in Your will, Father, not because it fits my pocket."

When I went to view the property, there was a white van on the drive but no trade signage, yet written in the dusty area were the words *Jesus loves you*. I had not entered the property at that point, but this was the one chosen by the Lord for me. No, the family were not Christians: the inscription was a joke from workmates because their colleague used to have a beard and long hair. I put in a lower offer than that recently advertised, and it was accepted.

3 A supply of information this time: I was on my way to Canada, the Lord having given the departure date three weeks previously. Because of the reason for the trip, a hotel or package deal was not appropriate, so I had not booked a place to stay in advance. The plane landed at Hamilton to refuel and take on extra passengers. A Canadian lady came and sat next to me, and we got chatting. I outlined my need for a couple of nights' board before moving on elsewhere. She informed me that when I had cleared customs, I should turn left and find a bureau managed by volunteers, who would telephone around on my behalf. The apparent difficulty was sorted, and I did not have to rely on a taxi driver to recommend his choice for a hotel: I would be much safer at the YWCA.

Prayer

Father God, You desire to be Lord of our finances and for us to be wise stewards. Sparrows cannot witness to Your salvation plan; You watch over us more closely than sparrows, and give us opportunities to share our resources with others, bringing You glory. Amen.

"For unto whomsoever much is given, of him shall be much required." (Luke 12:48)

10

Failures

Lest the reader surmise there has been a 100 per cent success rate in my Christian walk, this chapter will prove otherwise.

James 4:17 says, "Therefore to him that knoweth to do good, and doeth it not, to him it is sin." First Corinthians 10:12 concludes, "Wherefore let him that thinketh he standeth take heed lest he fall."

1 I was walking home, which was at the top of a steep hill at the time, with two bags of shopping. The day was hot, and as I passed a neighbour two houses from mine, she was unloading her car. The Lord said to me, "Speak to her about Me."

My reply was "She goes to church, and I am very tired." I may even have added the word *Lord* as well!

About six months later word reached me that she had had a brain haemorrhage and was in hospital dying. She was in her mid-thirties and had two young children. My repentance had to go deep, and I vowed with the Lord's help never to be disobedient again. I thanked Father God for Jesus' work on the cross, and the forgiveness and cleansing eventually came for me.

2 After having major stomach surgery, I wanted to regain my fitness, and having heard nothing to the contrary within church circles, I took up yoga (which is also one of the roots of Pilates practice). *Yoga* translates as "yoke"—that is, being yoked to foreign gods, which in this case would be gods from the eastern religions. In Matthew 11:29 Jesus said to be yoked to Him. Scripture says when we are made aware of the unrighteousness of our actions, then that knowledge brings us guilt (Leviticus 5:15–17), and we have to deal with the sin committed. But praise the Lord, we are on this side of the cross, and repentance and cleansing can be made, which I did.

3 Post the divorce I was finding it difficult to find re-employment, having just given up caring for my father. A Christian suggested that, as I enjoyed gardening, I should become self-employed in this type of work. I designed a flyer, and one afternoon delivered 400 of them to nearby homes.

A few days later my body showed all the symptoms of rheumatoid arthritis. The same friend drove me to the doctor for a blood test. Intercessors also prayed, with the resulting word from the Lord: because I had not signed off from receiving unemployment benefit at the same time that I had delivered the adverts for my new role, then these symptoms were the result. (My reasoning had been along the line that I would sign off when I had earned something.)

We serve a holy God, and I am sure He wanted to show me how "clean" we all need to be. I repented, and He said "I will heal you as you go." The blood test result came back negative. I had one reply from my adverts and booked a visit for a week ahead. The Lord did as He had promised, and all the symptoms disappeared. (As a postscript—the couple who were my first customers also had other agencies visiting for their circumstances, and word of mouth spread as these agencies visited other clients: I never had a need to re-advertise thereafter.)

4 During a visit to me, a married relative confided she had been trying to get pregnant for six months, and she became a bit tearful sharing this with me. When she had returned to her home, I questioned the Lord for the reason, as no one in the family line had had this problem before. "Well, you spoke it over her" was His reply.

He brought to my mind a memory when she was prepubescent and had stayed with me as a child. We had watched a comedy programme on the television together prior to her bedtime. The episode featured the wife of the comedian in a hospital to have her first baby. The chaos caused much laughter to us. However, this child relative took much longer than expected in the bathroom getting ready for bed. When I checked, she explained she was trying to have a baby. "You cannot have a baby," I said and then hurriedly I added, "not now anyway." The adult conversation she had just had with me, showed my pronouncement had come home to roost.

I would need to explain to a non-believer, and the Lord said I was to use the word *mindset* when I spoke to her next. When she next visited, I tentatively referred to the subject of the missing pregnancy. "I am sorry, I think I may have given you the wrong mindset due to what I said when you stayed with me" and specified the details to jog her memory.

She laughed and said, "Are you having one of your funny intuitions?"

"You could put it like that way" I replied, but her laughter and smile meant I had been forgiven. The next month she became pregnant.

In 1 Chronicles 4:9–10 Jabez is named by his mother with the expectation that he will cause more sorrow to others as he did to her in his birth. Yet Jabez appeals to the Lord (v 10) to change her prophecy.

Prayer

Father God, thank You for the salvation we have when we believe in the Lord Jesus Christ and repent of our sins, whether of omission or commission. Yet You know we are human and have times of weakness. Teach us more of Your ways, and give us an attitude ready to repent should we disobey Your instructions. Amen.

11
Truth

Father God loves His truth:

He guards His truth. Psalm 146:5–6 reads, "Happy is he that hath the God of Jacob for his help, whose hope is in the Lord his God: which made heaven, and earth, the sea, and all that therein is: which keepeth truth for ever …."

He does not change His truth or compromise it to fit in with the world's ways. Jude 3 exhorts us to "earnestly contend for the faith which was *once* delivered unto the saints" (emphasis added).

God does not lie. First Samuel 15:29 reads, "And also the Strength of Israel will not lie …." Numbers 23:19 adds, "God is not a man, that he should lie …."

God has an accounting system and a day of reckoning for sin. Ecclesiastes 3:15 says, "That which hath been is now; and that which is to be hath already been; and God requireth that which is past." (The note in the margin of my Bible says this could mean 'an account of that which is past'.)

God is faithful. He does not break a promise: 1 Kings 8:56 tells us that "there hath not failed one word of all his good promise, which he promised by the hand of Moses his servant."

God will bring us to Christian maturity. In Philippians 1:6 Paul says he is "confident of this very thing, that he which hath begun a good work in you will perform it until the day of Jesus Christ." When the Lord Jesus Christ said (John 14:7) He is the way, the truth, and the life, the first two should be our yardstick, through which we gain His life. And all this is because of His love for us before we believed in Him. As Romans 5:8 says, "God commendeth his love toward us, in that, while we were yet sinners, Christ died for us."

Further, *we need to choose His truth.* The example is found in Psalm 119:30:"I have chosen the way of truth: thy judgments have I laid before me."

Furthermore, *we ought to be valiant for His truth.* Jeremiah 9:3 condemns those who "are not valiant for the truth upon earth."

Truth protects us. Psalm 91:4 affirms, "His truth shall be thy shield and buckler."

Truth brings certainty. Proverbs 22:21 expresses the sage's purpose: "that I might make thee know the certainty of the words of truth …."

Truth leads to holiness. In Titus 1:1 Paul proclaims that his apostleship is according to "the acknowledging of the truth which is after godliness" (that is, not emotionalism). Though our emotions may be expressed at conversion, it is the grasp of the truth in God which is the final arbiter. James (1:18) declares, "Of his own will begat he us with the word of truth, that we should be a kind of first fruits of his creatures." Let us use the scriptures to get at the heart of God's truth (like the Bereans in Acts 17:11 who wanted to see from their scriptures "whether those things were so").

There's a Truth to be lived
and it's a gift.
There's a Truth to be lived
and it can't be earned.
There's no deserving
to get it, just a need for His Peace
at the time that He offers.
He'll be our focus,
not hocus pocus.
Known by Him as those who are trusting
thus we'll be bridal.
He's never tidal.
We'll forget all rivals.
Let's live this new Life,
within His sacrifice:
let that suffice,
nothing else will.
We'll be His, hidden by His safety net,
eternal security a reality.
He'll never leave, He's our "go'el"
so let us go tell
of His saving grace,
marked by His seal:
and thus to revel
living relationship with Him.
Let's not just the surface skim,
but jump in and swim.

There's a task He wants done –
to sow wherever He chooses.
He'll give the call,
and this call is for all
who follow His holy ways.
His Spirit empowers.
Let us wait if need be
till He causes us to flourish
with His designs where He plants,
safe in the knowledge
He knows where we are and in His care.
Our self life be subdued
to reflect Lord Jesus Christ's love
even under worldly pressure,
'cause thus diamonds are made.

(*go'el* = kinsman redeemer)

Prayer

Father God, may we see Your perspective on eternal issues, and respond by choosing this day whom we will serve (Joshua 24:15) and cling to You thereafter (Acts 11:23). May our faith be without wavering (Hebrews 10:23). We praise You for the new birth You grant via Your word of truth. Whatever the emotions we had in our conversion, we have a strong foundation on which to build when truth is paramount (Matthew 7:24–27). Help us to live Your way. Should circumstances be troublesome, please enable us to stand firm in our faith, because of the atonement which the Lord Jesus Christ achieved, and because of the Holy Spirit's empowering. Guard us against expecting our extensive praise to impress You, when no amount of praise will cover wrong attitudes (2 Samuel 6:5–7)—the ark of God was not carried in the prescribed manner, even though there was copious praise being given at the same time. Guard us, too, from being embroiled solely in good works, without a living relationship with You (Matthew 25:31–45—the parable of the sheep and goats). Amen.

12

Opposition

"To the intent that now unto the principalities and powers in heavenly places might be known by the church the manifold wisdom of God …." (Ephesians 3:10)

1 Ever thought why Proverbs 26 v 2 uses the pictures of a wandering bird (searching for food?) and a flying swallow (migratory?) to describe the working of curses? Both birds *do* land when they have found what they were seeking (in the same way, "the curse causeless shall not come").

I personally believe that a curse could land in a Christian's life, if it can find a weakness—in our armour, or possibly in sins which remain without repentance, or attitudes which are not godly; or even through ungodly images (e.g. tourist keepsakes) in our homes or minds. Hence the warning of Psalm 101:3 to "set no wicked thing before [our] eyes".

Causeless in my concordance equates to "for nothing"; that is, if a curse settles, there would be a reason: and *come* equates to "be brought". In the book of Ezekiel, the Holy Spirit departed progressively, even though ungodly practices were being carried out within His temple! The Spirit of God would normally have resided in the Holy of Holies (the westward end of the temple). However, in Ezekiel 8:3–4, His Spirit had moved to the north side of the temple; in 9:3 He had moved to the threshold of the temple; in 10:19 He left the threshold; and lastly in Ezekiel 11:23 He departed the city of Jerusalem altogether, to be on the mountainside. God will tolerate evil in His temple (our bodies, according to the New Testament) for only so long. Let us discipline ourselves in His word so that we do not spurn Him who gave His Son for us.

I believe a curse could affect any Christian. If it is suspected by its fruit, a heart search would be a good place to start. Praise God for the finished work of the cross and the gifts of repentance and forgiveness. Once the forgiving and repenting are done, the curse can be cancelled and mercy sought of the Lord for restitution of His goodness in us.

"And I will restore to you the years that the locust hath eaten …" (Joel 2:25).

Prayer

Father God, please keep us alert and mindful of possible enemy action against us; please also give us the explanation, so that we can take any appropriate action. Impress us with the use of the whole armour (Ephesians 6:13–18) and the use of the spear in 2 Samuel 23:6–7. [I believe that these "sons of Belial" would equate to those practising the occult today, and in order to come against their practices we need spiritual not natural weapons; our weapon would also need to be made of iron.] Would *iron* now equate with the sword of the word of God under the new covenant with the Lord Jesus Christ?

2 During a residential Christian course I attended, we were given teaching on how to countermand curses. A few days later I was due to hire a van to clear a rented property I had, so that I might accept the offer of joining the team at that Christian centre. A friend in the room next to mine would drive me to pick up the hire van, so that my own car would not be left in the hirer's compound over the weekend.

On the day of departure, as I left the bathroom, I felt a bit faint so I suggested we delay our departure, and I lay on my bed. It appeared that my face looked grey, so this friend fetched another student in the room opposite ours, a nurse who was also on the course. This nurse took my pulse and said I was having a heart attack. At that point I was certainly getting chest pains, which reverberated down both arms! "That is not in God's will for me; besides, look at the timing, and I do not have a heart problem." I had recently joined a local doctors' practice and had been given an all-clear on the health front.

When I asked the Lord what was behind this, He said it was voodoo. Mentally I scanned my room for any connecting objects. The first item He told me to destroy (with appropriate prayers as we had just been taught) was a piece of jewellery from my days in my previous home. After that, the intensity of the chest and arm pains decreased immediately by half. The other half left after

I destroyed a wall hanging I had made, again brought from my previous home.

These friends were amazed that I got up off the bed and announced we would resume our plan for the weekend: I promised to telephone the first friend when I reached halfway around the M25 (the major London Orbital route) when I arrived at a service station. Praise the Lord; He had defeated the enemy, and we can be aware of the devil's wiles (Ephesians 6:11) and the opposition (Zechariah 3:1).

3 On the day I was to move from the area where the above organization was situated, I found my car roof, windscreen, and bonnet covered with opened and flattened cardboard boxes. Someone was not happy! But now I had a procedure for dealing with ill-intent, and I took this route in my praying.

4 I became friends with another person I had met while at the Christian ministry centre. After a few years, this friend informed me she had found a Christian solicitor and had drawn up her own will. I asked for the name because I too needed to renew my own will. The solicitor was just setting up his practice and had no official cards but only draft ones. As I was then still living residentially as part of the team, he offered to keep the will safe on my behalf.

A year later, when I moved house on retirement from the organization, I informed him of my change of address for which I received an acknowledgement, with the notice that he too had moved.

A couple of years later, I wanted to change the executor of my will to someone closer to me, as the original person was now in another part of England. I looked on the Internet to trace the solicitor at his new address, but without success. Yet the Holy Spirit kept telling me, "There is a will."

I replied, "If I cannot trace the will, how is anyone else going to trace it if need be?" Finally, the penny dropped that I had been duped. A more local practice redrew my will. Obviously, I severed all links with the so-called "friend". Jude 4 says, "For there are certain men crept in unawares ..."; scripture also gives the solution, in Daniel 2:28: "But there is a God in heaven that revealeth secrets ...."

5 On a lighter note, I was in a Christian cell group one evening, and we were discussing creation. One of the attendees said she believed that we were developed from monkeys, and when God was satisfied these had progressed into humankind, we were given His life (Genesis 2:7). I replied "You would not be asking me to believe in a God who cannot get things right the first time, are you?" I later found out she was a biology teacher.

Prayer

Father God, thank You that the Lord Jesus declared, "It is finished" (John 19:30), and He now holds the keys of hell and death (Revelation 1:18). Enable us to live Christ-like lives and to wield the sword of the Holy Spirit, which is the word of God (Ephesians 6:17), so that thus the enemy's plans fail.

"And he answered, Fear not, for they that be with us are more that they that be with them" (2 Kings 6:16). Amen.

13
Angelic Help

"For he shall give his angels charge over thee, to keep thee in all thy ways." (Psalm 91:11)

By this quotation, I do not mean that we can seek in *advance* for an angelic appearance just for the sake of the experiential "buzz". Sometimes it is only with *hindsight* that an angelic visitation can be explained. If angels do cross into our lives, there would be a purpose.

1 My mother was in hospital undergoing tests. Leaving work early, I would visit and join my father and another family member at her bedside. As I arrived one time, she said, "Thanks for sending those men to see me". I enquired who. She replied, "They said you had sent them." She turned to the woman in the next bed and added, "You saw them too" — to which there was an affirming nod.

I asked "What did they look like?"

"They wore suits and carried briefcases." My mother then added, "They said they were from the Social, so you must have sent them because you work there too."

Then I understood — my mother had been an office worker,

and in the natural way of things, I had not sent them, but I had been interceding for her healing. "What did they say?" I queried.

"That everything would be all right." By now I believed she had had an angelic visitation, and they had been dressed in a way acceptable to her.

I ventured the comment, "All I can say is you must have had a visit from some angels then." That was all they had said to her; after which they left, walking out of the ward.

My mother received an "all-clear" medically.

2 I was in Canada with some spare time on my hands. I took a bus trip to a "living" museum where volunteers dressed in period costumes for the Bank Holiday weekend. Having completed my tour around, I stood at the bus stop to make the return journey. From the museum gate came another man to join me at the bus stop. I was feeling vulnerable at that time in my newly single status. He chatted away, obviously knowing from my accent that I was not a local. I was barely good-mannered, especially as he sat next to me in a near-empty bus. Halfway back to the town where I was staying, the bus broke down, and all passengers had to alight. There was quite a crowd. I did not know where we were, but the driver told us that another bus would be sent to collect us. Another bus did come along, and this man said it was for us. He was sticking to me like a limpet to make sure I got on, and no-one else came between us, he following as I got on. I thought, *I need to shake him off soon or he will see where I am staying.* I expected him to sit next to me again, he having had his own foot on the step to get on to the bus. But he did not — it seemed that he had disappeared; he was neither on the bus at all nor at the bus stop.

On reflection, I believe Father God knew of the impending breakdown of the bus and provided angelic assistance, as I was in a strange country.

3 We had a short break on one of the English islands. At the first meal, I scanned the room over the other guests. As my gaze rested on a couple to the side of us and facing the other direction, the Holy Spirit said, "Spiritualists." Just then, the lady turned and looked at me. The family member I was with had befriended the man sitting next to him at our own table, and a doubles snooker match had been arranged, with my own self making up the fourth member. However, the third member was to be the husband of the "spiritualist" lady.

My experience at snooker was definitely "past its sell-by date" although I could remember the sequence of play and the rules. Halfway through, the "spiritualist" wife came in to watch. In front of her I took aim for a shot where the black ball (the highest scoring one) would attempt to take in two angles where the targeted ball needed to recoil off each of two cushioned sides of the table. I watched in amazement as the black ball successfully negotiated the route and went down the chosen hole. This was not down to my skill; I must have had supernatural help.

The man who had arranged the match said. "I do not know what you are on, but it is good stuff."

"Do you want to know what it is?"

"No." We never had another match, and I am sure that the spiritualists went home wondering what had happened.

Prayer

Father God, thank You for Your angelic helpers, and the confirmation they bring to us that You are trustworthy. Amen.

14

Witnessing

"And ye shall be witnesses unto me both in Jerusalem, and in all Judea, and in Samaria, and unto the uttermost part of the earth." (Acts 1:8)

Because of the assurance we have that Father God is concerned about our everyday lives and is not willing that any should perish (2 Peter 3:9), we can be confident witnesses for Him, to believers (of His goodness in our experience) and to nonbelievers as well. He knows even the sparrows (Matthew 10:31), so He will be much more concerned regarding us.

1 Whilst I was in Canada and at the "living museum", the printed guide for that day indicated that there was a mock-up of a Masonic meeting room, up some stairs, and over another trade exhibit from days gone by. This mock-up was also open to the public. The guide said that the artefacts had been rescued from lodges that had closed. I climbed the stairs, and on nearing the top, I heard voices. I waited, as a family was before me, and I wanted privacy to witness, if such proved to be an opportunity.

The "lodge room" was entered at one corner and exited at

The Trustworthy God

the other. Between the public area and the main room, was a cordon roping off the public from entering further in and thus from touching anything. On the other side of the cordon from the public were two stewards with name badges.

I decided to play the confused female role. "I am a bit confused— I overheard what you said to that family before me: about who could be eligible to join. I do believe in a higher authority, am over eighteen years of age, but my higher authority already accepts me as I am without having to better myself under your system." (One steward was occupied at the back of the room, so all this conversation was only with the one before me.)

"Really?" the one in front of me replied.

I witnessed: "Yes, you see, I am a Christian, and my Lord Jesus Christ accepts me without all the hard work you had outlined to that family. He accepts me because of His grace, not because of my works." He blinked, and now he looked confused, and his fellow steward came over and tugged at his jacket sleeve. But I knew some snippet of what I had said had penetrated the Masonic veil. At the sleeve tugging, he triggered back into Masonic mode. I made a mental note of their two names for prayer purposes later. I also prayed for cleansing from the visit and from what I had seen.

2 I popped into a local supermarket. On the way out, another lady bumped into me pulling her own personal trolley. She apologized and explained she was not used to pulling the trolley, as she had had a frozen shoulder on the other arm due to an accident when … and she told me the whole story.

"I am a Christian. Would you like me to pray for you?"

She affirmed that was acceptable, and I asked Father God, in Jesus' name, to remove any shock of the accident and to heal her shoulder. She, in return, put her hands together in a prayerful gesture and looking upward said, "Thank You."

3 Over the garden fence a neighbour said to me, "It is 11.30 in the morning, so they got it wrong, did they not?" He was referring to the Inca prophecy in the news media that the end of the world would happen that morning.

"I am a Christian", I replied, "and my Bible says only God knows the timing for the end of the world. For me there is no point in worrying about it." We are still friendly.

4 Once when I was buying a car, the salesman needed my date of birth for the financial loan agreement. "Oh, that makes you a …" Here he mentioned a zodiac sign. "Well, I am sure I got it right for your date of birth," he retorted, after I had negated his comment.

I took up the challenge. "You may have got it right, but as I am a Christian, I do not believe in that system". He moved speedily on to complete the loan agreement.

Prayer

Father God, may we allow the Holy Spirit to give us boldness to speak of the Lord Jesus and the provision of salvation. Where we sow, may others water and reap. Thank you. Amen.

"I have planted, Apollos watered; but God gave the increase" (1 Corinthians 3:6–7).

15

Keeping Appointments

"Behold, to obey is better than sacrifice; and to hearken than the fat of rams." (1 Samuel 15:22)

1 Referring back to the time I had attended the six awareness trainings at the occupational college, the Holy Spirit told me one day on the way there, "When you take your lunchtime walk, turn right instead of left. I want you to tell someone sitting on a seat that they are loved by Me." I secretly thought that was a bit "twee". I had twenty minutes for that walk, so I planned a ten-minute walk away from the college and then a return, so as not to be late for my next session. I did pass a seat on the outbound walk, but there was no-one there. On my return walk there was an elderly lady on the seat. I sat down, and she asked me the time, which I gave her.

Then I said "I hope you do not mind, but as Christian I need to tell you that God loves you."

She replied, "That is good, because I have not been to church for six weeks, since I have just moved here and do not know the area. Could I come to your church?" I explained that I was attending day release at the college and lived a long drive away. I suggested she ring the local churches of some main denominations and explain her transport problem: whichever church offered to collect her and drive her home could be the one for her. My time had expired, and I explained I had to go. I hoped she found a loving fellowship.

2 I was due to attend a day conference in the Midlands (the middle of England), and I would be using the M1 motorway (freeway). The previous evening the Holy Spirit told me to leave at 5 in the morning instead of 7! At 6.30 in the morning I tried the first place for a break, but that did not open till 7 in the morning. The next one was open when I arrived.

In the ladies' washroom was a distraught and pregnant woman. I asked what the problem was. "Our car has broken down, and we have to get back to relieve the babysitter" was her reply. They did not have any arrangement with a mobile call out scheme for helping them. This was my "appointment" and why I had had to leave so early.

I drove the husband, wife, and male friend to their own home, much overshooting my own destination. When asked why I was so willing to help, I explained what God had told me, pointing out that He must have been concerned about them even before their car had broken down. I contacted the conference with a later arrival due to carrying out an errand of mercy.

3 Again, from my Canada trip, during my stay at the YWCA, an Asian young lady was at breakfast with us. Appreciating her possible vulnerability at eating the main meal outside the hostel,

I offered that she could accompany me to an inexpensive place (which I had come across for myself previously) to eat together. She agreed. Over our meal the Holy Spirit kept saying, "Talk to her about witchcraft." Oh help!

As we were staying in the YWCA, I asked if she was a Christian. Her reply was "No, I suppose I am a lapsed Buddhist."

I asked, "I thought people were born into Buddhism, so does one become lapsed?"

"I want to know who decides, when I die, what I would come back as. Clearly she believed in reincarnation. "Tell me in Buddhism do people put spells on other people?" – because I wanted to steer the conversation to where the Lord was leading me.

"Oh yes, they put pins in dolls to do that."

"What do people do for protection against that?"

"They make bigger spells."

I replied, "I do not have that problem. As a Christian, Jesus guides me and gives me His authority to deal with such things." As she was only staying one night and resuming her journey on to university the next day, I tore out the page on "Why We Need Jesus, and How to Become a Christian' from my daily reading notes and suggested she find the Christian Union at the university, who would answer any more of her questions.

4 On a holiday one summer, we were in Tenerife. Unfortunately, the resort and the timing of our holiday meant we were in a timeshare boom, and there were many representatives touting for business. I complained to the Lord. He replied "Speak to them about Me."

After the next representative had given his trade talk, I said

"You have had fifteen minutes of my holiday, so I request fifteen minutes of your time now."

I talked of the Christian faith, but he became defensive, saying, "I used to read my Bible, and my favourite book was Revelation."

I continued with "Revelation is not a cinema film show."

"I was born near Ealing Studios, where they made films."

I was not deflected. "If you want to get into Revelation, you will need a ticket. Why are you not reading the Bible anymore? With your 'gift of the gab', you ought to be a preacher." By now, he was getting a bit embarrassed, as was the unbelieving person I was with. "Anyway, I have used up the fifteen minutes of your time", and we parted.

However, from the next day onwards, not one representative approached us, whichever company they worked for; nor were we ever shunned. The representative I had witnessed to always waved and said 'hi' if our paths happened to cross.

Prayer

Father God, help us to grasp the love You have for the lost and to motivate ourselves to be Your witnesses. Guide us to those who have a need for a word from You in the season they are in. Remind us that time is running out for the witnessing to be done, as Jesus said in John 9:4. May You continue to water where we have sown. Amen.

16

Intercession

"Wherefore he is also able to save them to the uttermost that come unto God by him, seeing he ever liveth to make intercession for them." (Hebrews 7:25)

1 A family wedding was to be on a Saturday in April one year, and the long-range weather forecast on the previous Monday was for snow that Saturday. I prayed, asking the Lord for a bright and dry day despite the forecast and the family members agreeing with that forecast. The day itself broke fine and frosty (which soon thawed), and the weather was dry all day, with the sky so blue that the photos looked as if they had been taken on a summer's day.

2 Before the birth of a relative's second child, she was told that the baby was still in breech position five weeks before the due date. (One of my own children had been born this way, and it was explained to me at that time that the turnaround should happen at seven weeks before the due date.) "Father God, I thought You had broken this off our family line," I prayed.

"The baby does not know what to do," was His reply.

"There is only one Person who can tell the baby," I replied, and I proposed, "Would You send the Holy Spirit to the baby and tell it what to do, Father?" The baby turned around by the next check a week later.

3 My front kitchen window faced the road and also a junction. Some cars would drive past my home quite fast for a residential area. I prayed, "Please do not let there be any loss of life at this junction." The next day, a man was lying in the junction, and people were comforting him, while awaiting medical assistance. The medical assistance arrived, and he was taken for treatment.

4 A relative is a retained fireman. One evening in January 2015 I prayed against any enemy plan to cause widowhood to his family. Next day I had a call saying he had been taken to hospital for a check-up, due to a short period of concussion after the fire tender had overturned on a frosty bend. He sustained no lasting damage.

5 At one church, a married couple, who had just been accepted for fertility treatment, appealed for prayer that they would have a speedy conception. The Holy Spirit told me, and I shared this with a friend at the time, "There is no need. She is already pregnant, but it is too early to tell," which did prove to be the case. One lesson to be learned: check what the Lord wants, even though people may request what they think they need.

Prayer

Father God, thank You for the privilege of praying for others. May we give You all the glory when You answer our requests, rather than accepting self-promotion in the eyes of others. Keep us close to You so we can pray within Your will. Amen.

17
"Selfisms" Notes

"Rejoice, because your names are written in heaven." (Luke 10:20)

1 Revelation 2:1–7: The church at Ephesus had fading zeal.

2 Revelation 2:12–17: The church at Pergamos had false doctrines.

3 Revelation 2:18–29: The church at Thyatira tolerated a false prophetess.

4 Revelation 3:1–6: The church at Sardis was busy promoting their reputation.

5 Revelation 3:14–22: The church at Laodicea was run by the people rather than submitting to God—that is, by the popular vote (would this equate to humanism today?) and were thus hypocritical. [The two churches omitted from this list were the ones God commended.]

It is not only churches which can develop these characteristics.

We as individuals need to be on our guard too lest these traits come to us.

Let us check a few of these traits with the contrasting scriptures alongside:

1 Being selfish—Romans 12:10: "Be kindly affectioned one to another with brotherly love; in honour preferring one another …."

2 Wanting to increase our own self-esteem—2 Corinthians 10:12: "some … commend themselves: but they measuring themselves by themselves, and comparing themselves among themselves, are not wise."

3 Focussing on our own awareness—Hebrews 12:2: "Looking unto Jesus the author and finisher of our faith; who for the joy that was set before him endured the cross, despising the shame …." Our focus is to be on Him alone.

4 Self-pity — Trace the decline in King Saul from pitying himself down to bitterness and eventually to attempt the murder of David. Hebrews 12:15: "Looking diligently lest any man fail of the grace of God; lest any root of bitterness springing up trouble you, and thereby many be defiled …."

5 Self-indulgence—Galatians 5:24: "And they that are Christ's have crucified the flesh with the affections and lusts." John 3:30: "He must increase, but I must decrease."

Prayer

Father God, please renew us according to David's prayer in Psalm 51:10: "Create in me clean heart, O God; and renew a right spirit within me" – and according to Paul's admonition in Romans 12:2: "And be not conformed to this world: but be ye transformed by the renewing of your mind, that ye may prove what is that good, and acceptable, and perfect, will of God." Amen.

18

Notes on Salvation

1 We cannot earn our salvation. Ephesians 2:8–9:"For by grace are ye saved through faith; and that not of yourselves: it is the gift of God: not of works, lest any man should boast."

2 We cannot inherit salvation from our parents. Paul checked that Timothy had his own relationship with the Lord Jesus Christ. Second Timothy 1:5:"When I call to remembrance the unfeigned faith that is in thee which first dwelt in thy grandmother Lois, and thy mother Eunice; and am persuaded that in thee also …."

3 We cannot "catch" salvation like an illness or as an anointing from a gravestone. Luke 16:26:"Between us and you there is a great gulf fixed: so that they which would pass from hence to you cannot; neither can they pass to us, that would come from thence." This was said by the Lord Jesus Christ, and He never lies.

4 We cannot absorb salvation from a Christian environment. The thief on the cross next to the Lord Jesus Christ asked to be remembered when Jesus came into His kingdom. The Lord replied "Verily I say unto thee, Today shalt thou be with me in paradise" (Luke 23:43). The basis for this reassurance was only that the thief had recognized Jesus as his own Lord.

5 Salvation cannot come to us by some external ritual to the body. Baptism has an appropriate place after conversion. Romans 6:3:"Know ye not, that so many of us as were baptized into Jesus Christ were baptized into his death?" First Peter 3:21 "The like figure [Noah's ark] whereunto even baptism doth also now save us (not the putting away of the filth of the flesh, but the answer of a good conscience toward God,) by the resurrection of Jesus Christ." I do not believe it is possible for a baby to have an "answer of a good conscience toward God" or to grasp the resurrection of Jesus Christ.

6 The people we meet at a church could be so welcoming that we want to merge into that group. This would not be salvation, but rather it would be joining a social group and would appeal to our emotions. First Corinthians 1:17:"For Christ sent me not to baptize, but to preach the gospel: not with wisdom of words, lest the cross of Christ should be made of none effect." Thus, under these circumstances, the gospel would have no power to bring salvation.

7 Enjoying the worship music would not bring us salvation. First Corinthians 14:15:"I will sing with the spirit, and I will sing with the understanding also." An unbeliever might enjoy the worship music that appeals to his worldly nature, yet he cannot sing any spiritual songs with understanding.

8 Repeating a prayer at the end of a Christian book will not automatically bring salvation. The effectiveness of the prayer depends on the heart conviction at the time. Romans 10:9–10:"If thou confess with thy mouth the Lord Jesus, and shalt believe in thine heart that God hath raised him from the dead, thou shalt be saved. For with the heart man believeth unto righteousness, and with the mouth confession is made unto salvation."

9 Have you been through the Alpha course? John 16:8: "when he is come, he will reprove the world of sin, and of righteousness, and of judgment …." Thus, on the Holy Spirit day for this course, He would only bring conviction to nonbelievers, hopefully followed by repentance. And according to this scripture, the Holy Spirit would not first bring a "loving touch" to nonbelievers. There could also be the risk of peer pressure from other seekers for one to go along with the majority view. Should seekers report an esoteric experience, what would be the source of that experience in an unconverted life? According to Psalm 34:18, "The Lord is nigh unto them that are of a broken heart; and saveth such as be of a contrite spirit."

10 Joining an organization which requires you to keep that membership a secret will not bring true salvation. Some of these types of organization offer material benefits; however; according to Matthew 6:24, "No man can serve two masters: for either he will hate the one, and love the other; or else he will hold to the one, and despise the other. Ye cannot serve God and mammon."
Matthew 5:14: "Ye are the light of the world. A city that is set

on an hill cannot be hid." Our witnessing needs to be authentic, therefore duality of masters would negate this authenticity. Scripture says in Jeremiah 48:10, "Cursed be he that doeth the work of the Lord deceitfully …." Let us avoid God cursing us because of any hypocrisy.

11 Salvation cannot come by doing good works. We may be doing good works, but these should spring from our already-existing relationship with the Lord Jesus Christ. James 2:17: "Even so faith, if it hath not works, is dead, being alone."

12 Salvation has to be personal for each of us. The Queen of Sheba said "It was a true report that I heard in mine own land of thine acts, and of thy wisdom: howbeit I believed not their words, until I came, and mine eyes had seen it …."(2 Chronicles 9:5–6). Abraham had a personal relationship with God (see Genesis 12), as did Isaac; otherwise he could not have entreated God for Him to take away his wife's barrenness (Genesis 15:3). Jacob also had a personal relationship with God (Genesis 32:30).

At the time of our conversion or since:
    a) Were we convicted by the Holy Spirit of our sinful condition?
    b) Were we impacted by an impression of God's holiness?
    c) Did we repent?
    d) Was there fruit in keeping with that repentance (Luke 3:8)?
    e) Did we ask the Lord Jesus Christ to be in control of our lives?

Prayer

Father God, if anything was missing in our initial conversion, we give You permission to show us what that was. We also ask You to show us how to put the issue (if any) in line with Your perfect will for us. Amen.

19
Notes on Pride

"Pride goeth before destruction, and an haughty spirit before a fall." (Proverbs 16:18)

Pride brings its own harvest:

1 Destruction and a haughty spirit lead to a fall (Proverbs 16:18).

2 Whoredoms, sexual sin (Hosea 5:3–5).

3 Lack of God's wisdom, evil ways, and perverse speech (Proverbs 8:13).

4 Lack of empathy (is this what the unmovable scales of Job 41:15–17 represent?)

5 Persecutes the poor, boasts of its own desire, "blesses" those who are covetous and rebellious (Psalm 10:2–4).

6 Will be visible (as a crown in Isaiah 28:1 and as a necklace in Psalm 73:6).

7 Brings the rod or rule of foolishness (Proverbs 14:24—being under the rule of a crown).

8 Brings low (Proverbs 29:3).

9 Only has fellowship with those of the same outlook (Zephaniah 3:11).

10 Tramples under foot, either emotionally or socially (Psalm 36:11).

11 Is ambitious for its own self (Isaiah 9:9–10) and arrogant (Jeremiah 48:29).

12 Is devious and practises trickery (Isaiah 25:11).

13 Is self-blinkered as to the presence of pride (Psalm 59:12—the Lord acted quickly, and the proud people did not see His judgement coming).

14 Leads to idolatry (Leviticus 26:19).

15 Leads to hypocrisy, and imagines it has a god-like status (Ezekiel 28:17, and chapter 29).

16 Falsely accuses (1 Samuel 17:28).

17 Brings shame (Proverbs 11:2).

18 Causes division (Proverbs 13:10 "contention").

19 Starts small and grows like a plant if not dealt with (Ezekiel 7:10).

20 Thinks itself invincible, gloats, and is opportunistic for self (Obadiah 3).

21 Is not teachable (Daniel 5:22).

22 Follows worldliness (1 John 2:16).

23 Is possessive (Ezekiel 29:3).

24 Betrays and is unreliable (Ezekiel 29:6–7).

25 Bring false revelation or light (Isaiah 14 v.14 – and our Lord said our enemy always lies).

26 Brings desolation (Isaiah 14:17; see vss. 12–23).

27 Imprisons, either literally or socially etc. (Isaiah 14: 17).

28 Lastly, neglects God's people (Jeremiah 13:17).

In summary, pride is to be rejected by all Christians, but rather nipped in the bud. Second Chronicles 7:14: "If my people, which are called by my name, shall humble themselves, and pray, and seek my face, and turn from their wicked ways; then will I hear from heaven, and will forgive their sin, and will heal their land."

Isaiah 42:8: "I am the Lord: that is my name: and my glory will I not give to another …." This "other" would include a proud person. The only way to remove pride is to repent and ask God to remove it, followed by His cleansing.

Prayer

Father God, we can see that You cannot tolerate pride in Your followers. Please give us discernment to notice when pride wants to seduce and entice us; then give us the humility to deal with it. Amen.

20

Notes on New Age Practices

Hopefully, most believers will know when they break any of the Ten Commandments or are convicted by the Holy Spirit of having an ungodly heart attitude. However, when they sin inadvertently, the enemy will go before the throne of heaven to accuse them (Revelation 12:10). He does not accuse unbelievers, as they are already under his sway.

Yet for believers there is a way out under the New Testament. When we become aware of what we have done, or the Lord shows us, there is a remedy. Leviticus 5:15 says, "If a soul commit a trespass, and sin through ignorance, in the holy things of the Lord; then he shall bring for his trespass unto the Lord a ram without blemish out of the flocks …." For New Testament believers, Jesus has provided a way out via repentance because He was the perfect sacrificial lamb, having no blemish.

Sin is seductive, appealing to the flesh and emotions. Otherwise, where would the temptation be? A man is born again in his spirit (John 3—Nicodemus' conversation with the Lord Jesus Christ); yet a man's soul (flesh life) will need sanctifying after conversion via Christian discipleship. In our culture today, there are many therapies and practices of a deceptive nature, wanting to persuade us that they could something in which Christians can partake, appealing to the soul.

New Age teaching uses modern and pseudo-scientific language to market old and ungodly practices. In Deuteronomy 13:3, 6–8, God told the Israelites not to ask how pagan nations served their gods. Since we are grafted in (Romans 11:23), then the same applies to us.

Jeremiah 10:2:"Thus saith the Lord, Learn not the ways of the heathen, and be not dismayed at the signs of heaven; for the heathen are dismayed at them."

Listed below are some New Age practices, with the contradictory scriptures alongside:

1 *Wanting to know the future,* which uses divination to analyse problems or people (even to fathoming the sex of an unborn child), and dowsing to find hidden things. Psalm119:105: "Thy word is a lamp unto my feet, and a light unto my path." Where we need to know something in order to stop worrying, we will find the answer in the scriptures.

Prayer (for the reader to pray if need be)

Father God, I repent if I have done anything that comes within this category: please cleanse me of all their effects. Instead, I will trust You, Lord, with my future, and will trust You to reveal what is hidden, should I have a need to know. Amen.

2 *False religion and cults,* which falsely satisfy the need to have a "god". Ecclesiastes 3:11 says that God "hath set the world in their heart"; an alternate translation for "world" could be *eternity*.

Prayer (for the reader to pray if need be)

Father God, I repent where I have joined other religions or cults. Please cleanse me from all effects, and remove my name from their membership list. Thank You that You satisfy my need to worship (Romans 12:1–2) and that You are pleased when I offer You the sacrifice of a broken and contrite spirit (Psalm 51:17). Amen

3 *Ungodly entertainment or fundraising* (have you ever walked across hot coals to raise funds?). Much in the media titillates and seduces, and it is easy to go along with the culture of the world. Philippians 4:8 "Finally, brethren, whatsoever things are true, whatsoever things are just, whatsoever things are pure, whatsoever things are lovely, whatsoever things are of good report; if there be any virtue, and if there be any praise, think on these things." It was once heard from a pulpit: why would we seek entertainment through the things that crucified the Lord Jesus Christ?

Prayer (for the reader to pray if need be)

Father God, Your word says to delight ourselves in You (Psalm 37:4) and to be careful how we feed our minds and memories. Please alert us when we are tempted to succumb to the influence of the ungodly culture of the world around us, or when we are tempted to join others doing this. Help us to stand for Your truth in these dark days. Amen.

4 *Contacting the deceased.* Luke 16:26:"Beside all this, between us and you there is a great gulf fixed: so that they which would pass from hence to you cannot; neither can they pass to us that would come from thence." Deuteronomy 18:9–11:"thou shalt not learn … [to be] a consulter with familiar spirits, or a wizard, or a necromancer." When King Saul did this, the necromancer was shocked to discover that the real Samuel had appeared; she was expecting another type of spirit as had been the usual practice! God allowed Samuel to give Saul one final message. This one-off appearance should not be cited to justify necromancy, unless we too want to interact with unclean spirits.

Prayer (for the reader to pray if need be)

Father God, I cannot worship You in spirit and truth if I have pursued the ungodly practice of trying to contact the deceased. I repent where I have consulted them or have offered to consult them on behalf of others. Please break all connections with any deceased person and any spiritualist whom I have consulted. Where I have been an intermediary for others to do this for them, please break all these connections and destroy the seeds I may have sown in their lives. Cleanse me from all effects, and shut any door I may have opened to the astral realm. Amen.

5 *The use of spells*, which is really seeking to be in control instead of allowing God to be. This practice uses manipulation and includes beliefs in luck and superstitions. All this is rebellion to the word of God.

First Samuel 15:23:"For rebellion is as the sin of witchcraft …."

Prayer (For the reader to pray if need be)

Father God, I repent where I have practised this. I choose to believe Your word which says You are my protection (Psalm 9:9), and You are my strength (2 Chron. 33 v.6). Please cleanse from all effects of my sin, and nullify the fascination I have had. Amen.

6 Many of the above categories could also involve *altered states of consciousness*, as would hypnosis even for medical reasons. Second Peter 2:19: "for of whom a man is overcome, of the same he is brought in bondage." Christians need to have an active mind, not a passive one.

Prayer (for the reader to pray if need be)

Father God, I repent and ask You to forgive me for every altered state of consciousness I have experienced. If I have been passive and come under the influence of another person or organization, please sever the bonding to that person or organization. Cleanse me from all ill effects, and close any doorways I may have opened to the spirit realms. Amen.

7 *The use of visualization also influences the mind.* Picturing how one would like one's future to be falls into this category. Jeremiah 10:23: "O Lord, I know that the way of man is not in himself: it is not in man that walketh to direct his steps." Jeremiah 7:24 "But they hearkened not, nor inclined their ear, but walked in the counsels and in the imagination of their evil heart, and went backward, and not forward." Psalm 101:3: "I will set no wicked thing before mine eyes …" and this would include those things we imagine within our minds.

Prayer (for the reader to pray if need be)

Father God, please help me to watch out for and reject all mind games and day-dreaming. I repent where I have done this in the past and ask that You cleanse me from all ill effects. Amen.

8 *Have we sought to have more dreams than is usual?* Did we do this as a way of hearing from God? If He did not speak to us while we were awake, there would be a reason for His not speaking in the daytime. Manipulating the mind in order to have more dreams comes under divination. When the will is in passive mode and we are asleep, there could be an open invitation to enemy activity; and what would be the result of such a "dream"? Jeremiah 29:8: "For thus saith the Lord of hosts, the God of Israel; Let not your prophets and diviners, that be in the midst of you, deceive you, neither hearken to your dreams which ye cause to be dreamed."

Prayer (for the reader to pray if need be)

Father God, I repent where I have participated in this practice. I ask that You cleanse me from all dreaming which falls outside Your will for me, together with all the implications. Please disconnect me from the source(s) where this teaching was given, and cleanse me from the effects of those sources. Amen.

First Thessalonians 5:21:"Prove all things; hold fast that which is good."

21

The Need for Ongoing Repentance

Our sins separate us from God. Isaiah 59:2 says, "But your iniquities have separated between you and your God, and your sins have hid his face from you, that he will not hear." Praise God, Jesus shed His own blood for us. Romans 3:25: "Whom God hath set forth to be a propitiation through faith in his blood, to declare his righteousness for the remission of sins that are past …." Hebrews 9:22: "and without shedding of blood is no remission."

What is the cost today for us? That cost is repentance. Let us listen to scripture, lest we be deaf to the call from our Lord Jesus Christ to repent when we need to. Hebrews 3:13: "But exhort one another daily, while it is called Today; lest any of you be hardened through the deceitfulness of sin."

Prayer (for the reader to pray if need be)

Father God, please help us live holy lives, and help us listen to the Holy Spirit more so that we will not be deaf to any need for daily repentance. Amen.

22

Finale

Flint-like Christ strode to His cross
To save mankind from being lost
And in order to show Satan who's boss.

Lord Jesus Christ's coming back again
To gather His own and end our pain
Of living in this world of stain.

Before it's too late may we all say yes
To His invitation to be blessed
With eternal salvation and His praiseful rest.

So gather your wits and examine the truth
('though past gone may be your youth).
What do you lack in the way of proof?

He's the Redeemer and Mediator with God.
He'll never be bested if in His footsteps you trod.
He's still waiting just for your nod.

Taste and see what difference He'll make
When all your sins you forsake
And Him your Saviour and Master you make.

Whilst researching my mother's family tree, I discovered there was a crest with a motto, but this information had been lost in the passage of the years and had not been referred to by the immediate forebears.

Genesis 49:24:"[Joseph is] the shepherd, the stone of Israel."

The family motto was "May the stone prove true."

And I believe He has proved true, and to Him be all the glory. Amen.

Author Description

Pat has been married and has three children and five grandchildren. Now retired from professional life, she has been called of God to be a writer of Christian books. She has also spent seven years in the healing and deliverance ministry. She is a keen gardener, growing her own fruit and vegetables. She attends a Pentecostal church.

Lightning Source UK Ltd.
Milton Keynes UK
UKHW03f1532210318
319832UK00001B/67/P